WHAT SHALL I BE?
A CHAT WITH YOUNG PEOPLE

BY THE
REVEREND FRANCIS
CASSILLY

"And every one that hath left house, or brothers, or sisters, or father, or mother, or wife, or children, or lands for My name, shall receive a hundredfold, and shall possess life everlasting." (Matt. xix: 29)

NEW YORK
THE AMERICA PRESS
1914

IMPRIMI POTEST

A. J. BURROWES, S.J.

Provincial Missouri Province

NIHIL OBSTAT

REMEGIUS LAFORT

Censor

IMPRIMATUR

JOHN CARDINAL FARLEY

Archbishop of New York

LETTER TO THE AUTHOR
FROM REVEREND A. VERMEERSCH, S.J.

Louvain, le 23 février, 1914.

Mon Révérend Père: P. C.

Votre petit livre me plaît extrêmement. Il expose une doctrine très solide avec une merveilleuse clarté. D' une lecture agréable, il intéressera la jeunesse des écoles, et l'encouragera à faire un choix généreux d' état de vie. J' estime que, traduit en flamand et en français, il ferait également du bien à nos collegiens de Belgique.

Votre dévoué en N. S. et M. I.
A. Vermeersch.

TRANSLATION

My Reverend Father:

Your little book pleases me exceedingly. Its doctrine is very sound and set forth with wonderful clearness. It makes pleasant reading, and will interest the young of school age, and encourage them to make a generous choice of a state of life. In my opinion, a Flemish and French translation would also be profitable to our college students in Belgium.

Devotedly yours in Our Lord and Mary Immaculate,
A. Vermeersch.

**TO THE THOUSANDS
OF TRUE-HEARTED BOYS AND GIRLS
HE HAS BEEN BLESSED TO KNOW
OF WHOM
SOME ARE GONE TO HEAVEN**

AND MANY ARE BATTLING FOR THE RIGHT
IN THE SANCTUARY
THE CLOISTER OR THE WORLD
AND WITH ALL OF WHOM
HE HOPES ONE DAY TO BE REUNITED
FOREVERMORE
IN GOD'S OWN COURTS
THIS LITTLE BOOK
IS AFFECTIONATELY DEDICATED
BY THE AUTHOR

PREFACE

In this little book the writer has aimed to present, in brief and simple form, sound principles which may assist the young in deciding their future course of life. The subject of vocation, as it is called, has suffered much, during the last two or three centuries, at the hands of rigorist authors, who so hedged the approach to religious life with difficulties and restrictions, as to frighten or repel many aspiring hearts from it.

Great stress was laid by these writers on the special interior attraction, by which God was supposed always to manifest His call, so that no one might legitimately enter the state of perfection, unless he felt this unmistakable impulse from within. And on the other hand, given this evidence of the Divine predilection, to disregard it was a sinful preferring of one's own will to God's, which, in all likelihood, would be attended with grave consequences for this world and the next.

Spiritual writers of the last decade have been rereading the Fathers and great Theologians upon this subject, and as a result the cobwebs of misconception are being swept away. The Reverend A. Vermeersch, S.J., of Louvain, deserves the gratitude of all for his lucid and convincing treatment of religious vocation, in his "De Religiosis Institutis et Personis" (Vol. II, Supplement III; also Vol. I, P. 4, C. I), where he clearly shows from Scripture, the writings of the Fathers and leading theologians, the true nature of the invitation to the evangelical life. The reader is also referred to the article on "Vocation," by the same author, in the Catholic Encyclopedia.

Another document throwing light on the subject, is the Decree of July 15, 1912, framed by a special commission of Cardinals appointed to examine the work of Canon Joseph Lahitton on "La Vocation Sacerdotale." This Decree, approved by the Holy Father, contains the following passage: Vocation to the priesthood "by no means consists, at least necessarily and according to the ordinary law, in a certain interior inclination of the person, or promptings of the Holy Spirit, to enter the priesthood. But on the contrary, nothing more is required of the person to be ordained, in order that he may be called by the bishop, than that he have a right intention, and such fitness of nature and grace, as evidenced in integrity of life and sufficiency of learning, which will give a well-founded hope of his rightly discharging the office and obligations of the priesthood." This Decree does away, at once, with the special spiritual attraction, always and essentially required by so many for vocation to the priesthood.

It may not be rash to conclude, in a similar way, of a religious vocation "that nothing more is required of the person who is a candidate for religious life, in order that he may be admitted to the novitiate by the lawful superior of an order, than that he have a right intention, and such fitness of nature and grace required by the order, as will give a well-founded hope of his rightly discharging the obligations of the religious life in that order."

The present treatise aims at no more than putting in form suitable to the young the sound conclusions of such reliable authors as Father Vermeersch, Canon Lahitton and Rev. P. Bouvier, S.J.

As to the advisability of priests, parents and teachers fostering and developing in the young the desire of a religious life, the words of St. Thomas are positive: "They who induce others to enter religion, not only commit no sin, but even merit a great reward." (Summa, 2a, 2æ, Quæst. 189, art. 9.)

And the Third Council of Baltimore, urging priests to develop vocations to the priesthood, says: "We exhort in the Lord and earnestly entreat pastors and other priests diligently to search after and find out, among the boys committed to their care, those who seem suited and called to the clerical state. If they find any boys of good disposition, of pious inclination, of devout and generous minds, and able to learn; who give promise of persevering in the sacred ministry, let them nourish the zeal of such, and sedulously foster these precious germs of vocation." (Paragraph 136.)

Priests, teachers, confessors and others who have dealings with the young, will find it very practical to have at hand several copies of some reliable booklet on the priesthood and religious life, which they may give or lend, as occasion offers, to promising boys and girls. Such books will, at least, make their readers think, and God's grace frequently acts through the medium of the written or spoken word.

Creighton University, Omaha,
Easter Sunday, 1914.

CHAPTER I
GETTING A START

Youth is the dream time of life. It views the world through the prism of fancy, tinting all with rainbow colors. It lives in a creation of its own, where it rules with magic wand, conjuring into its realm the beautiful, the heroic and the magnificent, and banishing only the prosaic and commonplace. To the youthful dreamer, every ruler is all-powerful, every soldier brave, every fire-fighter a hero, and every editor a wizard, at whose nod the news of the world flies to the huge cylinder presses, and then flutters away in white-winged sheets through town and country.

But gradually, the stern realities of life forcing themselves on the maturing mind, it realizes that it must choose from the various activities that make up the sum of human existence. The thoughtful boy and girl then begin to ask the question, "What shall I be?" or "What shall I do?" The various walks of life spread out before them like a maze of tracks in a railway station, all leading away in dwindling perspective to the witching land of the unknown.

An ambitious boy views with delight the various professions, and pictures to himself in turn the great deeds and triumphs of the soldier, the statesman, the lawyer, the physician, the architect, and finally perhaps the electrician, who plays with the lightning and harnesses it to the ever-extending service of mankind. All these are votaries of noble avocations, and he who excels in any one of them is a hero, and a benefactor of his kind. Every occupation which is useful to the human race, which contributes to the sum of man's comfort and happiness, is laudable and worthy an intelligent being. St. Paul was a tent-maker by trade, and he gloried in the fact that, even during the days of his apostleship, he was not a burden to others, but supported himself by the labor of his hands.

Life pursuits rank in dignity and worth, according to the perfection or benefit they bestow upon the worker himself, and his fellow-man. Far above the artisan or husbandman, who occupies himself with the material needs of his neighbor, with providing him food, raiment and shelter, rise the teacher, writer and professional man, who minister to the needs of the mind. And highest, perhaps, of natural callings is the conduct of the government, which gives peace, order and happiness to entire nations.

But not every pursuit is suited to all dispositions, nor can any one hope to excel in all trades and professions. The strength of body and skill of hand required of a mechanic may be lacking to a professional man, and the long years of study and experience demanded of a physician are possible to but few. Nature destines some for a life of action and adventure, for the command of armies or the conquering of the wilderness; others it dowers with literary tastes, or the power to thrill an audience or guide a State.

3

No one is necessarily tied down to any special occupation of life. According to your disposition and character, your ability and inclination, education and training, you are free to select any sphere of action within your reach and opportunity. But this very freedom of choice sometimes leads to mistakes. One without the proper temperament or ability, lacking in patience and sympathy, and unable to make a diagnosis, aims to be a physician, and he becomes only a quack. Many a one, who aspires to direct the destinies of the State, achieves only the station of a political subordinate or spoilsman. And one whom nature destines for the free and independent life of a farmer, often sentences himself to life imprisonment behind the "cribbed and cabined" desk of a counting house.

Perhaps the most frequent mistake of young people is to tear themselves away from school, where they have the opportunity to prepare themselves for the higher positions of life, and by so doing deliberately limit themselves to a life of mediocrity. They have an ambition, but a false one. Eager to enter, though unprepared, the arena of life and accomplish great deeds, they lack the student's patience and industry, which would crown them in after years with the laurel of success.

Be ambitious then, my young friend, aim high in life; endeavor to achieve something great for yourself and for mankind. You will have only one life in this world, then make the most of it. Take advantage of your opportunities. Attend school as long as you can, because generally the greater your knowledge and learning, your training and preparation, the higher and wider the career that will open before you.

All legitimate pursuits of life have been illustrated and adorned by numberless Christian heroes and heroines, who served God, sanctified themselves, and brought glory to the Christian name by their fidelity to duty. Would you be a soldier? Could there be more glorious names than those of St. Sebastian and St. Martin; the Crusader, Godfrey de Bouillon, and the Grand Knight of Malta, de la Valette?

Do you long to ride the ocean waves, and brave the tempest? What more heroic predecessor would you have than the great "Admiral," the navigator and discoverer, Columbus? If your ambition be to sit in the councils of State, to steer your country safely through breakers and shoals, fix your gaze on Sir Thomas More, Daniel O'Connell, Windthorst or Garcia Moreno—Christian heroes all.

CHAPTER II
AIMING HIGH

In a garden are flowers varying in hue and form and size. The roses blow red and white and pink, scenting the air with their myriad petals, the lilies lift up their delicate calyxes to the wandering bee, the perfumed violets hide their modest heads in beds of green, and the fuchsias sway from their stems in languid beauty. But varied as are the flowers in charm, each is perfect of its kind. No artist could improve their tints nor trace truer curves; no carver chisel more delicate or finished forms.

And God's Church is a spiritual garden, where bloom souls varying in every virtue, charm and grace, and all breathing forth the good odor of Christ. In it are school-boys, gentle maidens, devoted mothers and fathers of families, rich and poor of every nation and clime, of every station and calling. God made them all; He loves them all, and on each He has grafted the bud of faith, which will blossom forth into all supernatural virtues.

God also wishes each one in His garden to be perfect of his kind. Jesus, sitting on the Mount of the Beatitudes, and teaching the multitudes that were ranged on the grass about Him, bade them "be perfect as also your heavenly Father is perfect." (Matt. v: 48.) [1] This, then, is the perfection Christ expects us to aim at, the perfection of God Himself, in Whom there is nor spot nor wrinkle. He will not be satisfied with us, so long as low aims, imperfect motives, disfigure our souls and stain our conduct.

As St. Paul says in his letter to the Ephesians, God chose us before the foundation of the world to be "holy and unspotted in His sight." (Eph. i: 4.) In fact, St. Paul, whenever he addresses the Christians, calls them "saints" because every Christian man, woman and child, is expected to be holy, holy in the grace of God, in conduct, in thought and act, at every time and place. Every Christian must be sacred, a shrine wherein dwells the Divinity, and whose doors must be closed to everything profane. "Know you not, that your members are the temple of the Holy Ghost, who is in you, whom you have from God; and you are not your own?" (I Cor. vi: 19.) Your soul, then, my child, is holy, consecrate to God, and into it must enter nothing defiled, nothing savoring of the world, its maxims and principles. Keep your soul pure as the roseate dawn, clear as starlight and bright as the sun.

"Every one of you," said Christ Himself, "who doth not renounce all that he possesseth, cannot be my disciple." (Luke xiv: 33.) This seems a hard doctrine, for who would be able to give up all he has, parents, home and possessions? There are occasions when the love of God and the love of creatures come into conflict; and when this occurs the true disciple of Christ will not hesitate. He will fearlessly sacrifice everything, even life itself, rather than forsake his Creator. The martyrs did this. St. Agnes gave up suitor, home and wealth, and laid down her innocent young life, to become the spouse of Christ. The boy Pancratius faced the panther in the arena, and the yells of a bloodthirsty mob, rather than abjure his faith; and so won a martyr's crown.

Perfection then is our destiny. In heaven we shall attain to it, and in this life we should begin to practice it. If we would have God's love in its fulness, if we would always be worthy to nestle in His bosom, to feel the arms of His affection drawn close about us, we must never sully our conscience with the least taint of sin. For all the world we would not offend our parents, and God is to us in place of father and mother and all. He is the infinitely perfect; He is love and beauty and tenderness itself, and His absorbing desire is to reproduce similar qualities in us.

But how are we to be perfect? By always doing His holy Will, as we see it and know it, to the best of our ability. Christ issues the clarion call to all Christians, to take up their cross daily and follow Him. He who always does his best, and, obeying the dictates of conscience, walks by faith and charity in all his actions before God, and conducts himself in all circumstances of life according to the principles of faith and reason, is living up to the Divine call, and striving after perfection.

"But are there any such persons in the world?" some one may ask. "They say that there is nothing perfect under the sun, and this time-honored adage, no doubt, applies to persons as well as to things." It is true that very few are perfect in the sense that they sojourn in the world, unmoved, like the angels, by the least ruffling of passion. But there are many, very many, pure, holy souls, who aim constantly at perfection, and who attain to it substantially; for day by day, year in and year out, they keep themselves from the guilt of serious sin, and delighting to carry out God's will in all their actions, frequently draw nigh the Tabernacle to commune in heavenly raptures with their Love "behind the trellis."

Nor is the number of these elect souls limited to any one calling or profession, for they are found in the seclusion of home, in the crowded mart, in the stress of business and professional life. When the week-day Mass is over in the parish church, and the little band of devout worshippers descend from the church steps, would one not say that there is a look of heavenly peace upon their countenances, a peace that overflows to their features from the deep well-springs of charity within? No legitimate walk of life, then, is alien to perfection. All Christians are urged to it; and many attain to it. They use the things of this world "as though they used them not," their hearts are free from undue attachment to the possessions of earth, and they go through life as pilgrims to their final home; and should God be pleased to reward their constancy by sending them trials and sufferings, they will come forth from the ordeal like pure, refined gold.

[1] While this text refers primarily to the perfection of forgiving enemies, it is applied also by commentators to perfection in general, for the reason that it is closely connected with the preceding and following exhortation of Our Lord to many and various virtues. And even if the text were limited expressly to one virtue, the fact that God's children are urged to the perfection of this virtue because it is found perfectly in their Heavenly Father, would seem to imply that He, so far as imitable by creatures, is the measure and standard of their

perfection, and hence, as He is the All-Perfect, that they too should strive to be perfect in all virtue.

CHAPTER III
THE STATE OF PERFECTION

Speaking one day to the multitude, Our Lord likened the Kingdom of Heaven "to a merchant seeking good pearls, who, finding one pearl of great price, went away and sold everything he had and bought it." (Matt. xiii: 45-46.) What is this precious pearl that so charmed the merchant as to make him sacrifice all he had to gain possession of it? It is doubtless the true Church, or faith in Christ, but theologians apply the parable also to the highest union with God by charity, or Christian perfection. Perfection, then, may be called this lustrous pearl, more precious and radiant than any which gleams in royal diadem. You may buy it, but the price is the same to all. You must offer in exchange all that you have, keeping nothing back. Are you willing to make the bargain?

There have been many Christians throughout the centuries who were enamored of this perfection. They sighed and longed for it, but, alas! the conditions in which they lived, the temptations that lay about them, the cares of raising a family and struggling for a livelihood, so engrossed their attention and seduced their affections, that they almost despaired of living entirely for God, and thus attaining perfection. A young man of high aspirations one day came to Jesus, and asked Him what he must do to gain eternal life. The Master replied, "Keep the commandments." But the young man was not satisfied with this; he wished to do something more for heaven, as we learn from his reply, "All these have I kept from my youth; what is still wanting to me?" Then Jesus spoke the memorable words that have echoed down the ages, "If thou wilt be perfect, go sell what thou hast, and give to the poor . . . and come, follow me." (Matt. xix: 21.)

The questioner, so the Scripture records, went away sorrowful, for he had great wealth. He was willing, no doubt, to give alms and bountifully, but to sacrifice all his possessions and live in poverty—this was beyond his generosity. Christ's advice, however, has not fallen by the wayside. Theologians tell us that in His brief words Our Lord indicated the evangelical life, which He elsewhere explained more fully, bidding the youth become poor and then come and follow Him in perfect chastity and obedience (Suarez, "De Religione," lib. iii, c. 2).

The teaching thus presented by Christ has never been fruitless in the Church. Myriads of chosen souls, more magnanimous than the young man, have heeded the Saviour's admonition and hastened to sacrifice all for His sake. The nature of the evangelical life—so called because taught in the "Evangelium," the Latin word for Gospel—consists in the practice of the three counsels, voluntary poverty, perfect chastity and obedience. And why is the exercise of these three counsels so excellent? Because by them a Christian parts with everything that is most pleasing to mere nature. By poverty he renounces his possessions and the right of ownership; by perfect chastity, the pleasures of the body; and by obedience, his free will. Could one do more than to give up everything he owns, and then complete the renunciation by dedicating his body, aye, his very soul, to Christ? Nothing is left that he may call his own. He is a stranger in the world, without home, parents or family, money or earthly ties; he is all to God, and God is all to him.

While a person may be in the *way* of perfection, by observing the counsels privately, with or without a vow, if he takes perpetual vows in a religious order or congregation approved by the Church, he is in what is called "the *state* of perfection," or "the religious state." The vows give a final touch to the holocaust in either case, since by them he offers all he has and is and is forever, so that it becomes unlawful for him to retract his offering. He who exemplifies all Christian virtues to a high degree of excellence, according to his condition of life, may be called perfect, and to this perfection all Christians are called. But, religious, that is, they who live in the religious state, bind themselves by *profession* to aim at living a perfect life. They have heeded Christ's invitation, "If thou wilt be perfect," and engaged themselves, under the sanction of the Church, to the obligation of striving for perfection.

No one could claim that all religious men and women are actually perfect; but they are in the state of perfection—that is, by virtue of their state and profession they are bound to the observance of their vows and rules, which observance, in the course of time, will be able to lead them to the attainment of such perfection as weak mortals, with God's grace, can hope to acquire in this life. In response to Christ's exhortations, we find throughout the world to-day a great army of religious men and women, white-robed Dominicans, brown-garbed Franciscans, followers of St. Benedict, St. Augustine, St. Alphonsus, St. Vincent de Paul, and St. De la Salle, the Blessed Madeleine Sophie Barat, Julie Billiart, Jean Eudes, and of numerous other saints, who, under the standards of their varied institutes, march steadily in the footprints of the lowly Nazarene, Who had not whereon to lay His head.

The ambitious Christian boy and girl, then, will aim at doing their best, and must, if they desire close companionship with Christ, strive after perfection, for such is the Master's desire. But should a youth have further ambitions, and say to himself, "I desire to distinguish myself in God's service, to lead for Him a life of action and achievement, wherein my exertions will bring amplest returns for eternity," will he refuse to consider the life of the counsels? Will he not rather ask himself whether this manner of life is practicable, and possibly even meant and intended for him? Choose then, my young friend, your sphere of life but deliberately and carefully, remembering that on your decision will largely depend your greater happiness in this world and the next.

CHAPTER IV
WHO ARE INVITED?

The boy or girl who is deliberating on a future career will naturally ask, "Who are invited to the higher life? Is the invitation extended to all, or limited to the chosen few?"

Let us try to find out the answer to these questions. One day the disciples of Our Lord having asked Him (Matt. xix: 11-12) whether it were not better to abstain from marriage, He replied, "All men take not this word, but they to whom it is given. . . . He that can take it, let him take it." St. Paul also writes to the Corinthians (I Cor. vii: 7-8), "I wish you all to be as myself, . . . but I say to the unmarried . . . it is good for them, if they so continue, even as I."

Now, let us examine these passages, according to the interpretations of the Fathers and Doctors of the Church, so that there will be no danger of reading a wrong meaning into them. There is question in both texts of abstaining from marriage, of advising the unmarried not to marry, which, of course, is equivalent to advising them to practice perpetual chastity. St. Paul says clearly and forcibly that he would desire all to remain unmarried like himself. However, in the next verse he exempts from his advice those who do not control themselves. What does he mean by this? There are some who have strong passions, or who by self-indulgence have so strengthened their lower nature and weakened their will-power, that lifelong continence seems beyond them. Such persons, therefore, who know from experience that they will not overcome temptation and sin, or who find the struggle too hard to continue, he advises to marry.

We may now inquire whom Our Lord meant by those "to whom it is given." Does He mean that the power of practicing virginal chastity is given only to the selected few or to the many? St. Chrysostom, interpreting His words, says that this gift of chastity "is given to those who choose it of their own accord," adding that the "necessary help from on high is prepared for all who wish to be victors in the struggle with nature" (M. P. G., t. 58, c. 600). [1] St. Jerome tells us that this gift "is given to those who ask it, who wish it and labor to obtain it" (M. P. L., t. 26, c. 135). St. Basil explains that "to embrace the evangelical mode of life is the privilege of every one." (M. P. G., t. 32, c. 647.) To the sophistical objection that if all persons practiced virginity marriage would cease, and so the human race would perish, St. Thomas (Summa, 2a 2æ, Quæst. 189, art. 7) gives the reply of St. Jerome, "This virtue is uncommon and desired by comparatively few"; and then adds, "This fear is just as foolish as that of one who hesitates to take a drink of water, for fear of drying up the river."

Can it be said, then, that every boy and girl, with the exception noted by St. Paul, is advised and exhorted to preserve virginal chastity throughout life? To understand aright the answer to this question, we must remember that there are two general courses of life, the married and the unmarried, open to all; every person necessarily being found in the one or the other. And each individual of the race is privileged to make a free and voluntary choice of either condition; no one having the right to interfere with this personal liberty, by forbidding or prescribing wedlock to any properly qualified person.

Both these states have been created by God, and both are His gifts to man. The nuptial tie, elevated to the dignity of a sacrament, is likened by St. Paul to the union existing between Christ and the Church. "A prudent wife," says the Book of Proverbs (xix: 14), "is properly from the Lord." Whoever marries "in the Lord" performs a virtuous act, and the Church, to show her appreciation and approbation of it, invests the wedding contract with a rich and hallowed ceremonial. They, then, who wed do something pleasing to God; but they who, for virtue's sake, forego their natural right of marrying, make an offering still more grateful to Him.

This is the doctrine in the abstract. But in its application to individual cases we find some so situated, so hampered by their own temperament and disposition, or by actual conditions about them, that a life of perfect continence seems impracticable for them. One, for instance, who yearns for the safety and seclusion of the cloister, and yet sees its doors closed against him for some reason, feels himself constrained to take refuge from the storm and stress of the world in the sanctuary of marriage. On such persons the Creator does not impose a burden above their strength. Wishing us to be happy and content even in this life, as well as the next, He asks of us here only a "reasonable service."

Guided by these principles, the great majority of the faithful in all ages have deemed it prudent and expedient for them to marry. And the wisdom and prudence of their choice God approves and commends. For His Providence manifests itself to us in all the events and circumstances of life, dwelling alike in the fall of the leaf and the roll of the wave, and speaking to our hearts by the voice of all creatures. While, then, external or internal impediments may prevent some from hearkening to Christ's call, and their own will may deter others, His invitation of *itself* does not exclude any; it is general, ever waiting for those able and willing to accept it.

But does not a person have to feel a special call before binding himself to perpetual chastity? To answer this let us suppose that one is considering the advisability of daily attendance at Mass or of total abstinence from intoxicating liquor. In themselves these are good works and under proper advice a person might engage himself to their performance. Grace would be required for them, as for every other act of supernatural virtue, but no one would say that to assume such obligations a special call from heaven is prerequisite. Now, chastity is governed by the same laws as other virtues, by the same laws as mortification, alms-deeds and works of charity. Every virtuous act requires two things, the grace and the will to cooperate with the grace; and these two are also the only requisites for the exercise of continence; a special inspiration being no more necessary for it than for perpetual abstinence from meat or spirituous liquors.

Lifelong virginity is, of course, a higher, nobler and more far-reaching virtue than the others mentioned, but it involves no special personal call. If this were required, in addition to the general invitation of Scripture, the doctrine of the Fathers that all are invited could scarcely be true. If all are invited, then he who wishes must have the power to accept the invitation. If two calls are necessary, one general and the other particular, he who has only the first may be said to have only half an invitation, which seems very absurd, and certainly is contrary to the practically unanimous teaching of the Fathers.

St. Thomas tells us: "We should accept the words of Christ which are given in Scripture as if we heard them from the mouth of Christ. . . . The counsel (to perfection) is to be followed by each one not less than if it came from the Lord's mouth to each one personally. (Opusc. 17, c. 9.) And even granted that the devil urges one to enter religious life, it is a good work, and there is no danger in yielding to his impulse." (Opusc. 17, c. 10.)

Taking these words of the Angelic Doctor for our guidance, we realize that the invitation and exhortation of St. Paul is general, that it embraces all unmarried persons who feel the well-grounded hope within them that with God's grace they can live up to it.

We may go further and say that, as St. Paul was speaking not his own doctrine, but the doctrine of Christ, which is unchangeable, it applies equally to-day. So one who is convinced that no obstacle, except his own will, prevents his acceptance of the Apostle's advice, can readily imagine Christ standing before him and saying, "My child, you should be more pleasing to Me were you to remain unmarried for My sake." If Jesus Christ really stood before you, dear reader, and thus addressed you, what would be your reply? There can be no doubt that it would be prompt and in accordance with His wish. You would say, "If God so loves me as to make a suggestion to me, as to sue for my undivided heart, I shall be only too glad to give Him all I have, to make any sacrifice for His sake." But God does speak thus, through the mouth of the Apostle, to all who are "zealous for the better gifts."

Now, what says your heart? Will it reject the special love Christ offers? He says, "I give you the choice of two gifts, matrimony or virginity; virginity is by far the more precious—but take which you wish." Will you be so irresponsive as to reply, "Give me the lesser gift; Thy best treasures and best love bestow on my companions"?

Speak thus if you are so minded. God will love you still; but can you be surprised if He cherish other generous souls more? Take or reject virginity as you like. It is yours for the taking, but if you reject it do not say, "I have no call, no invitation to the higher life." You have the invitation now, in common with other Christians; and the great-souled ones are they who accept it, for "many are called, but few are chosen."

It may now be asked whether what has been said about the observance of chastity applies also to poverty and obedience. Spiritual writers tell us that the full and entire evangelical life includes all these three counsels, and that the principles on which one rests are common to all. Christ in His call invites those who are not hindered by insuperable obstacles, to follow Him in the practice of all the counsels, the reason for all being the same, namely, to sacrifice everything for His sake. It is evident, however, that there may be more hindrances to the observance of all three counsels than to the keeping of only one. Some religious orders, for example, on account of their special work, may demand from applicants health, or youth, or talent, or learning, or other qualifications, which every person does not possess. For community life, too, a peaceable temper and agreeable manners are usually necessary. Moreover, one may be so bound by obligations of justice and charity to his parents or others, that he cannot leave them. [2] The general principle, however, is fixed and sure, that the clarion call to the practice of the counsels is in itself general, and applicable to all who are not hindered by circumstances or impediments from accepting it. No further special invitation is necessary. You who are free have the invitation—take it if you wish.

[1] This and similar references are to the Migne edition of the Greek and Latin Fathers.

[2] It may still be possible, however, for a person who is prevented from entering community life, to practice the counsels while living in the world.

CHAPTER V
DOES CHRIST WANT ME?

Said a boy one day, "How in the world does a person ever know he is to be a priest?" This little lad was a budding philosopher: he wanted to know the reason of things. But many an older person has been puzzled by the same question. Some boys and girls, having a distorted notion of the nature of a vocation, imagine that Almighty God picks out certain persons, without consulting them, and destines them for the priesthood or religious life, whereas all other persons he excludes from this privilege. In other words, they think God does it all.

Of course, we know there is an overruling Providence, Who watches over all His creatures, and particularly over His elect, distributing His graces and favors as He wills, and bringing all things to their appointed ends. If, for instance, a boy is blind, and for this reason no religious congregation will accept him, it is apparent that God does not design him for the religious life, though even for him the private practice of the counsels might still be open.

But we must not imagine that God settles everything in this world independently of our free will. He wishes us not to steal, but we may, if we choose, become thieves. Two boys of the same qualifications, let us say, have the general invitation of the Scripture to a life of perfection; they both have the same grace, which one accepts and the other rejects. What makes the vocation in the one case? The action of the boy himself in choosing to follow the invitation. And why has not the other boy a vocation? Because he declines to correspond with the grace. God does His part; He issues the call to all who are free from impediment and hindrance. Any one who wishes can accept the call and thus, in a sense, make his own vocation, for God's necessary help is ever ready to hand for those who will use it.

We may here remark that, while the practice of all virtue comes from man's free will, it also springs in a higher and greater degree from God, the author of grace. Without Him we can do nothing. "Who distinguisheth thee? Or what hast thou that thou hast not received?" asks St. Paul (I Cor. iv: 7). God's grace must necessarily precede and accompany every supernatural action. In a very true sense, while a religious may say: "I am such voluntarily of my own free choice," he must also admit, "I am a religious by the grace of God, Who prepared me, aided me by external and internal helps, enlightened my mind and strengthened my will to embrace the life He designs for me."

In much the same way, a daily communicant may say: "It is of my own accord and wish that I receive daily, but it is God's predilection that has prompted me to this design, given me the opportunity and strength of purpose to carry it out, and keeps me faithful to it, so that it is by His grace and Providence that I am a daily communicant." Countless others could adopt the same practice, were they not too sluggish or indifferent to ask for or correspond with the grace of doing so.

Most ordinary vocations have several stages of development. Very many persons, with all the qualities required for the evangelical life, and unimpeded by any obstacle, begin to consider, under the influence of grace, the advisability of embracing that kind of life. This may be called the remote stage of a vocation. One who finds himself in this condition of mind, if he prays for light and guidance, is faithful to duty and generous in the service of God, may be enabled by a further enlightenment of grace to perceive that this life is best for him, and consequently that it will be more pleasing to God for him to adopt it, and finally he may decide to do so. Such a one has a proximate vocation, the only further step required being to carry out his purpose. This decision, be it observed, is the result of the action of his free will, aided by efficacious grace, which is a mark of God's special love.

A little illustration may assist us to get a clearer idea of the matter. Suppose Christ were to walk into your class-room, how would He act? Would He pick out four or five pupils and say, "I wish you to be religious, the others I do not want, and I forbid them such aspirations?" Do you think our loving, gentle Redeemer would speak in this harsh way? And yet some good, but ill-informed Christians think this a faithful representation of God's method of action in this important matter.

How, then, would Christ really address the class? He would say, "My dear children, I want as many of you as possible to follow closely in My footsteps, to become perfect. I should be glad to have all of you, who are not prevented by some insuperable obstacle, such as ill-health, lack of talent, home difficulties, or extreme giddiness of character. I hope to have a large number of volunteers." How many children in that class-room, do you think, would joyfully hold up their hands, and beg Him to take them?

Now, this is truly the way God acts with the individual soul. He comes to it perhaps not once only but repeatedly, and makes the general offer, using for this purpose the living voice of His minister, or the written page, or a prompting impulse from within. And when God's desire is so manifested, all that the soul needs is to cooperate with grace, if it will.

That this interpretation of the general call of Scripture to a higher life is in accord with sound doctrine, we can perceive from St. Thomas, who says that the resolution of entering the religious state, whether it comes from the general invitation of Scripture or an internal impulse, is to be approved. And in his "Catena Aurea," commenting on St. Matt. xix, he quotes St. Chrysostom, who holds that "the reason all do not take Christ's advice is because they do not wish to do so." The words "to whom it is given," according to this Greek father, show that "unless we received the help of grace, the exhortation would profit us nothing. But this help of grace is not denied to those who wish it."

This is also the teaching of St. Ignatius in his "Spiritual Exercises," where he designates three occasions in which to elect a state of life: the first, when God appeals to the soul in some extraordinary way; the second, when grace moves the heart by consolation and desolation, and the third, when the soul without any special motion of grace, "that is, when not agitated by diverse spirits, makes use of its natural powers" to elect the state of life which seems best suited to the praise of God and the salvation of one's soul. Evidently a vocation decided in the last-mentioned time, implies no special call beyond the general scriptural invitation and the determination to accept it.

Some one may ask how it is then that so many virtuous boys and girls, endowed with all needful qualifications, prompt and ready to respond to the suggestions of grace, yet have no efficacious desire of the higher life. It is not for us to search into the secrets of hearts, nor to penetrate into the mystery of grace and free-will. The Spirit breatheth where He wills, and God distributes to each man his own proper gift. But, at least, one thing seems certain, that many fail to recognize God's will, because they expect it to be manifested in some extraordinary or palpable manner. Perhaps, too, they have prepossessions against it, they have already marked out their own career, they never think about the counsels, or pray for guidance. If all our young people only realized that Christ's invitation is general and meant for them, provided no impediment exist, and they wish to embrace it; if at the same time they kept their hearts free from worldly amusements, and applied themselves to prayer and self-control, volunteers in greater number would rally to Christ's standard.

CHAPTER VI
"I FEEL NO ATTRACTION"

Some boys and girls, with hearts of gold, have often said: "I feel no attraction for the higher life. I appreciate it, admire it, and yet I fear it is not for me, as I have no inclination to it. If God wanted me, He would so perceptibly draw me to Him that there could be no mistaking His designs."

Almighty God is wonderful in His ways, and He "draws all things to Himself," but by methods varying as the temperaments and characteristics of the human soul. Sometimes He speaks to His chosen ones in thunder tones, as when He struck down St. Paul from his horse, on the road to Damascus, saying from heaven, "Saul, Saul, why persecutest thou me? . . . It is hard for thee to kick against the goad." (Acts ix: 4.) Again He speaks in gentle accents, as to St. Matthew, the publican, when he sat at his door taking customs, saying to him, "Follow me!" At other times He seems silent and indifferent, standing quietly by, letting reason and conscience argue within us, and point out our line of action.

There is what is called vocation by attraction, and also such a thing as vocation by conviction. Some of the great saints from earliest childhood felt a strong, irresistible charm in the higher life; they were drawn by the golden chain of love to the cloister. "I have never in my life," said a boy, "thought of being anything but a religious." Some young people have no difficulty in making up their minds to follow Christ, their whole bent of thought and character being for the nobler life. Like Stanislaus, they ever say, "I was born for higher things." It was such a precocious disposition of heart that led St. Teresa to foreshadow her saintly career when, as a little girl, she ran away from home to become a hermit.

But feeling is not always a trustworthy guide, either in temporal or spiritual matters; reason, slow but sure, is generally much safer. You feel the fascination of worldly things, of company and society, fine clothes, luxuries and comforts, the dazzling stage of life with its applause of men. Is that a sign God destines you for worldly vanities? Quite the contrary, for all Christians are warned against the seductions of the world and the flesh; and the life of the counsels is essentially a constant struggle with nature and its allurements. "The kingdom of heaven," we are told, "suffers violence, and the violent bear it away."

If the following of Christ were easy and agreeable to the senses, where would be the merit and reward of it? Just in proportion as it involves effort and the overcoming of natural repugnance, does it become high and sublime. "Do not think," says Our Lord (Matt. x: 34), "that I came to send peace upon earth: I came not to send peace, but the sword. For I came to set a man at variance with his father, and the daughter with her mother. . . . He that loveth father or mother more than me, is not worthy of me."

Natural antipathy then to the higher life, far from indicating that God does not want us, merely shows that the inferior powers of the soul are striving against the superior. In fact, when this aversion becomes pronounced, it is sometimes evidence of a keen strife going on within us between nature and grace, which could scarcely happen unless grace were endeavoring to gain the mastery by winning us to Christ.

"But," it may be objected, "if nature rebels, does not God always give a counter supernatural attraction to those whom He calls, so as to smooth the way before them?" Certainly God gives the necessary grace to perform good actions, but grace is not always accompanied by sensible consolation. Suppose a boy is chided by his parents for a fault and he is tempted to deny it; but overcoming the suggestion he admits his wrong-doing and expresses sorrow for it. In this he acts bravely and with no sense of accompanying satisfaction, since the pain of his parents' displeasure is so keen as to overcome for the moment any other feeling. His action is prompted simply by the conviction of duty.

Accordingly, if a young man knows and clearly sees that he has every qualification for the religious life, and has even been told so by a competent adviser; if he has sufficient talent and learning, a steady disposition and virtuous habits, and the persuasion that the duties of this state are not above his strength; in short, if he is convinced that there is no obstacle, save his own will, between him and the higher life, can he truly say, "I feel no inclination to such a career, and therefore, I have no vocation"? Such a person, of course, is free to say, "I will not enter religion," because there is no obligation incumbent upon him to this state, but he cannot justly say that God withholds from him the opportunity or invitation to do so. He has already what is called a remote vocation, as was explained in the fifth chapter, and what he needs is a clearer vision and alacrity of will, which he may have good hope of obtaining by earnest prayer and a generous and insistent offering of self to the disposal of the Divine good pleasure. For Our Lord Himself tells us: "All things whatsoever you ask when ye pray, believe that you shall receive, and they shall come unto you." (Mark xi: 24.)

Remove then, my dear young friend, from your mind that false and pernicious notion, which has been destructive of so many incipient vocations, that because you feel no supernatural inclination or sensible attraction, you are not called of God.

In general, it is sufficient that the aspirant to religious life be free from impediments, and be desirous of entering it. For eligibility to a particular religious congregation the applicant must be fit, that is, he must have the gifts or endowments of mind, heart and body which that institute demands; his desire to enter must be based on good and solid motives drawn from reason and faith, and he must have the firm resolve to persevere in the observance of the rule. When to this subjective capacity is added the acceptance of the candidate by a lawful superior, his vocation becomes complete.

The requisites, then, are three, two on the part of the applicant, namely, fitness and an upright intention, and one on the part of the superior, the acceptance or call. Nothing more, nothing less is required. If any one of these three essentials is wanting, there is no vocation to that particular institute.

It is worthy of observation, however, that these qualifications of the applicant need be fully evident only towards the end of the novitiate, when the time comes for taking the vows and assuming the obligations. To enter the noviceship, as a rule, much less is required, though even for this preparatory step a person must have the serious intention of trying the life and discovering whether it is suitable to him, and there should be a reasonable prospect of his developing the needful qualifications.

For spiritual directors, then, to regard a vocation as something exceeding rare and intricate, to subject the candidate and his conscience to searching and critical analysis, to harassing cross-examination and prolonged tests, as though he were a criminal entertaining a fell project, to endeavor to probe into the secret workings of grace within him, is only to cloud in fatal obscurity an otherwise very simple subject.

A high-souled youth or maiden may still be deterred by the thought, "I now see that I have all the necessary qualifications for the higher life, and hence may embrace it if I choose, but I fear it will be too difficult for me to carry the yoke without sensible devotion or consolation." In answer to this, we must remember that a hundredfold in this world and life everlasting in the next are promised to those who leave all to follow Christ. In this hundredfold are included many privileges and favors bestowed by God upon His chosen spouses. Make the effort, overcome nature, decide to embrace God's offer, and you will find yourself overwhelmed by a deluge of spiritual consolations, which God has been withholding from you to try your generosity and courage; you will experience the truth of Christ's words, "My yoke is sweet, and my burden light." Sensible consolations, in fact, nearly always follow the performance of a virtuous act, but seldom do they precede it. A hungry person, before sitting down to table, may feel cross and out of humor, but as soon as he begins to partake of the generous viands a feeling of genial content and satisfaction with all the world steals over him.

It would, of course, be an error for any one to think that of his own natural powers he could observe the counsels; since this, being a supernatural work, demands strength above nature. But he who feels helpless of himself, should place his entire trust and confidence in God's grace and assistance, saying, with the Apostle, "I can do all things in him who strengthened me" (Ph. iv: 13).

Come, then, to the banquet prepared for you by the great King. Regale yourself with the spiritual viands set before you, and not only will you be strengthened to do God's will, but transported beyond measure with spiritual delights.

CHAPTER VII
"SUPPOSE I MAKE A MISTAKE?"

A young man once exclaimed to a friend, "Suppose I make a mistake! I could not bear the disgrace of leaving a religious order after entering it." Having wrestled with this thought for some time, he finally determined to try the religious life, with the result that after taking the habit, he was too happy to dream of ever laying it aside.

However, it is not wrong, but highly prudent, for any one to consider whether he has the courage and constancy to persevere. Religious life is not a pathway of roses. It is meant only for true men and valiant women, not for soft, languid characters, nor for fickle minds, which change as a weather vane. Marriage also is a serious step, for it brings much "tribulation of the flesh," and so he who would enter on it must earnestly consider whether he can live up to the obligations it entails. But because marriage has many cares and responsibilities, is that a prohibitive reason against embracing it? A soldier's life, too, is hard, and a farmer's; in fact, all pursuits and vocations in this world have their sombre side. But he who would win success in any career must be ready "with a heart for any fate" to meet and overcome all the trials and hardships that await him.

On one occasion Our Lord made use of the following parable (Luke xiv: 28): "Which of you having a mind to build a tower, doth not first sit down and reckon the charges that are necessary, whether he have wherewithal to finish it: lest after he hath laid the foundation, and is not able to finish it, all that see it begin to mock him, saying, 'This man began to build and was not able to finish'?" This parable Our Lord seems to apply to those who have the call to the Faith, and He concludes with the words, "So likewise every one of you that doth not renounce all that he possesseth, cannot be my disciple."

But His advice is also applicable to one who contemplates a closer following of Christ by the pathway of the counsels. Certainly, by all means, deliberate before taking any step of importance in this world. Never act on inconsiderate impulse in any matter of moment, but weigh carefully the obligations you are to assume, and consider whether you have sufficient strength of character to persevere in any good work you are undertaking.

Still, when all is said and done, it remains true that timidity is not prudence, nor cowardice caution. Nothing great was ever accomplished in this world without courage. Prudence and caution may be overdone, and easily degenerate into sloth and inactivity. In a battle he who hesitates is lost, and life is the sharpest of conflicts. Had Columbus wavered, he would not have discovered America. Close followers of Christ must be brave and noble souls, willing to risk all, to sacrifice all in the service of their leader. If you are excessively timid and fearful of making a misstep in your every action, it is a fault of character, and unless you overcome it you will never do great things for yourself or others.

When reason and conscience point the way, plunge boldly forward, trusting to the Lord for all the necessary helps you may need to carry out your designs. He will never desert you when once you enlist under His flag. When it comes to "supposing," there is no end to the dreadful things that *might* happen, but never *will*. Little children have a game called "supposing," each one making his supposition in turn, but even they do not anticipate that their creations of fancy will ever prove true. A man once said: "I have lived forty years, and have had many troubles, but most of them never happened," meaning that he had often anticipated and dreaded evils which never came to pass.

Let us, however, grant that occasionally a novice leaves his order: is that such a disgrace? By no means; he, at least, deserves credit for attempting the higher life. He is far more courageous than many Christians who are too timorous even to try. After all, what is a novitiate for, if not to discover whether the candidate has the requisite qualities? And judicious superiors will be the first to advise a young man or woman to leave, if he or she has wandered into the wrong place.

There is, moreover, a danger on the opposite side that wavering souls often fail to take into account. What if they make a mistake by not entering religious life? Is it better to err on the side of generosity to God, or on the side of pusillanimity? If one make a mistake by entering religion he can easily retrace his steps before it is too late, but once he commits himself to worldly obligations, he can seldom break their fetters; and many a man, when overwhelmed with the cares and anxieties of life, has regretted, when all too late, that he had not hearkened to the voice of grace that invited him to the calm and peace of the cloister.

St. Ignatius thus forcibly expresses the same thought: "More certain signs are required to decide that God wills one to remain in the secular state, than that He wishes him to enter on the way of the counsels, for the Lord so openly urged the counsels, while He insisted on the great dangers of the other state." (Directory, c. 23.)

The devil, who employs every ruse to wreck a vocation, has one favorite stratagem, which unfortunately succeeds only too often. When he cannot induce a person to give up entirely the idea of following Christ closely, he frequently induces him, under a variety of pretexts, to postpone its execution. If he can get the person to wait, to delay, he feels he has scored a victory, for thus he will have ample opportunity to lure his victim to a love of the world, to present the vanities of life in such enticing colors, as finally to withdraw him altogether from his first purpose. This disaster, unfortunately, is only too common, and many a one finds out, to his cost, that unseasonable delay has destroyed in him the spiritual savor, and made shipwreck of his vocation.

If, then, you see clearly it is best for you to tread the pathway of the counsels, go boldly on without delay or hesitation, and if difficulties loom big before you, they will fade away at your approach, like the fog before the sun; or, if they remain, you will be surprised at the ease with which you will vanquish them, for when the Lord is with you, who will be against you? You will be guarded against possible rashness in choosing the higher life by consulting a prudent director or confessor, at least, so far as to get his approval of the step you propose to take. For the knowledge such a one has of the secrets of your conscience gives him a specially favorable opportunity to judge whether you have the virtue and determination of character to persevere in the pathway of the counsels.

CHAPTER VIII
"THE WORLD NEEDS ME"

Some young people endeavor to persuade themselves that as the world needs good men, they can better serve Church and State by remaining in the secular life. The world, of course, does need good men and women, and it has them, too; but even if there were a dearth of good Christian laymen, is that any reason for you to refuse God's invitation and sacrifice your own spiritual advancement and happiness in order to help others? Our first duty is to ourselves. Are we to be so enamored of benefiting others as to forego God's special love, and to rest satisfied with a lower place in heaven? God invites you to Him, and you turn away to devote yourselves to others, who perhaps care little for you, and will profit less by your example.

And, moreover, once absorbed in the business and cares of life, you may find yourself, like most others, so preoccupied in your own personal advancement, in providing for yourself and those dependent on you, that scarce a thought remains for the interests of your neighbor. And thus your initial high resolve may soon sink to the low level of beneficent effort you see in others. Selfishness, to a large extent, rules in the world, and how can you promise yourself that you will escape its grasp? He certainly is rash who thinks he can, single-handed, contend against the world and its spirit.

No doubt many men and women of the world are devout Christians, and in a thousand ways spread about them the good odor of Christ. Countless brave Christian soldiers, upright statesmen, kings and peasants, matrons and maids, are the pride of Christianity for what they have done and dared in behalf of their neighbor. All honor to the virtuous laity throughout the world to-day, who by their edifying lives, their sacrifices for the faith, their unwearying industry, and fidelity to Mother Church, are sanctifying their own souls, and assisting others by example, counsel and charitable deed.

But for every layman that has distinguished himself by heroic devotion to the welfare of his neighbor, many religious could be mentioned who have done the same. We have all heard of Father Damien, who banished himself to the isle of Molokai, where the outcast lepers of the Sandwich Islands had been herded to rot and die; and there taking up his abode, soon changed the lepers, who were living like wild beasts, without law or morality, into gentle and fervent Christians. Having no priest as a companion, he on one occasion rowed out to a passing steamer, which was not allowed to land, to make his confession to a bishop aboard. And while he sat in his row boat, because forbidden to climb into the vessel, and shouted his sins to the bishop on the deck above, the passengers looking curiously on, he certainly must have been a spectacle to men and angels. And his sacrifice became complete when he contracted the leprosy from his people, and thus gave up his life for his flock.

Nor is this a solitary instance of such magnanimity. A short time ago, when a Canadian bishop entered a convent and called for volunteers to start a leper hospital, every nun stood up to offer her services. You have heard of the great Apostle of the Indies, St. Francis Xavier, who is said to have baptized more than a million pagans. St. Teresa, the mystic, was not prevented by her cloister and her ecstacies from helping her neighbor, for she founded a large number of convents, both for men and women. Blessed Margaret Mary was only a simple nun in the Visitation Convent of Paray-le-Monial, yet God chose her to make known and spread the great devotion of the Sacred Heart, a devotion which has brought more comfort and consolation to sorrowing humanity than the combined philanthropic efforts of a century. God took a gay cavalier, whose only ambition was to wear foppish clothes and thrum a guitar, made him into a friar, and bade him found the great Franciscan Order, whose glorious works for mankind cannot be enumerated.

And if we ponder the nature of religious life, the marvels accomplished by simple religious cease to astonish us. One who devotes the major portion of his time and attention to a definite object will certainly attain great results. Now, most religious seek their own sanctification in concentrating their energies on the welfare of their neighbor, in ever studying, working, planning for his betterment. The love of God, as shown in charity to others, is the absorbing purpose of their life. On the other hand, the man of the world must generally care first and foremost for himself and family, and only the time he has left, incidentally as it were, can he bestow upon others.

This point is thus forcibly expressed by St. Paul (I Cor. vii: 32-34): "He who is unmarried is solicitous for the things of the Lord, how he may please God. But he who is married is solicitous for the things of the world, how he may please his wife; and he is divided. And the woman, unmarried and a virgin, thinketh on the things of the Lord, that she may be holy in body and soul. But she who is married, thinketh on the things of the world, how she may please her husband."

15

The works of the religious orders are varied and numerous. Some care for the outcasts of society, some for the sick or the old, the orphan and the homeless; others, leaving the comforts and conveniences of modern life, cheerfully face the danger and hardships of remotest lands to bring the light of the Gospel to pagan nations. More than a million Chinese to-day are fervent Christians, and to whom do they owe their faith under God? To religious missionaries. The Benedictines of old spent their lives in the pursuit of learning, and in teaching barbarous tribes the art of husbandry. The glorious Knights Templar were a militant order; and the members of the Order of the Blessed Trinity for the redemption of captives, the first to wear our national colors of freedom, the red, white and blue, sold themselves into slavery for the release of others. Scarcely a want or need of the human race has not been provided for by some religious body.

But probably the most common pursuit of religious bodies in our day is teaching. Hundreds of thousands of religious men and women, in all lands whence they are not banished, spend their lives in the class-room. And the reason for this preference is the extraordinary demand for schools in every direction. The young must be taught, and Holy Mother Church knows only too well that religious training must be woven into the fibre of secular learning if we would not have a conscienceless and irreligious generation. So she issues her stirring appeal for volunteer teachers, and a vast multitude of religious have responded in solid phalanx. Some one has said that if all the sisterhoods were taken out of our schools in the United States, we should soon have to close half our churches.

Religious, then, are carrying on vast and important works for the benefit of the Church and society. Many other services which they render might be mentioned, such as preaching and hearing confessions, the publication of books and periodicals, the cultivation of the arts, science, literature and theology. But enough has been said to show that they are leading a strenuous life, and that boy or maid, who is emulous of heart-stirring deeds, could scarcely find a more propitious field of action than in the religious state.

CHAPTER IX
MUST I ACCEPT THE INVITATION?

It is not the purpose of the writer to exaggerate, to frighten or coerce persons into religious life, by holding out threats of God's displeasure to those who refuse, or by citing examples of those whose careers were blighted through failure to heed the Divine call. It is His desire rather to imitate Christ's manner of action, portraying the beauty and excellence of virtue, and then leaving it to the promptings of aspiring hearts to follow the leadings of grace.

Christ, all mildness and meekness as He was, uttered terrible denunciations against sin and the false leaders of the people; but nowhere do we read that He denounced or threatened those who failed to accept His tender and loving call to the life of perfection. To draw men's hearts He used not compulsion, but the lure of kindness and affection.

Our Lord sometimes commanded and sometimes counselled and between these there is a difference. When a command is given by lawful superiors it must be obeyed, and that under penalty. God gave the commandments amidst thunder and lightning on Mount Sinai, and those commandments, as precepts of the natural law, or because corroborated in the New Testament, persist in the main to-day, and any one who violates them, refuses to keep them, is guilty of disobedience to God, commits a sin. But when Christ proclaimed the counsels, He was merely giving advice or exhortation, and hence no one was obliged to follow them under pain of His displeasure. Suppose a mother has two sons, who both obey exactly her every command, and one also takes her advice in a certain matter, while the other does not; she will love the second not less, but the first more. So of two boys, who are both favorites of God, if one accept and the other decline a proffered vocation, He will love the latter as before, but the former how much more tenderly!

Moreover, God loves the cheerful giver. By doing, out of an abundance of charity and fervor, what you are not obliged to do, you gain ampler merit for yourself, since you perform more than your duty, and at the same time you give greater glory to God, showing that He has willing children, who bound their service to Him by no bargaining considerations of weight and measure. But if, through fear of threat or punishment, you make an offering to God, your gift loses, to an extent, the worth and spontaneity of a heart-token.

Some think that not to accept the invitation to the counsels, is to show disregard and contempt for God's grace and favor, and hence sinful. But how does a young person act when he declines this proffered gift? He equivalently says, with tears in his eyes, "My Saviour, I appreciate deeply Thy invitation to the higher life; I envy my companions who are so courageous as to follow Thy counsel; but, please be not offended with me if I have not the courage to imitate their example. I beg Thee to let me serve Thee in some other way." Is there anything of contempt in such a reply? No more than if a child would tearfully pray its mother not to send it into a dark room to fetch something; and as such a mother, instead of insisting on her request, would only kiss away her child's tears, so will God treat one who weeps because he cannot muster courage to tread closely in His blood-stained footsteps.

The young have little relish for argumentative quotations and texts, but it may interest them to know that Saints Basil, Chrysostom, Gregory Nazianzen, Cyprian, Augustine and other Fathers all speak in a similar strain, holding that, as a vocation is a free gift or counsel, it may be declined without sin. [1] The great Theologians, St. Thomas, Suarez, Bellarmine and Cornelius a Lapide also agree on this point.

But putting aside the question of sin, we must admit that one who clearly realizes that the religious life is best for him and consequently more pleasing to God, would, by neglecting to avail himself of this grace, betray a certain ungenerosity of soul and a lack of appreciation of spiritual things, in depriving himself of a gift which would be the source of so many graces and spiritual advantages.

Do not, then, dear reader, embrace the higher life merely from motives of fear—which were unworthy an ingenuous child of God—but rather to please the Divine Majesty. You are dear to Him, dearer than the treasures of all the world. He loves you so much that He died for you, and now He asks you in return to nestle close to His heart, where He may ever enfold His arms about you, and lavish his blandishments upon your soul. Will you come to Him, your fresh young heart still sweet with the dew of innocence, and become His own forevermore? Will you say farewell to creatures, and rest upon that Bosom whose love and tenderness for you is high as the stars, wide as the universe, and deep as the sea? Come to the tender embraces of your heavenly spouse, and heaven will have begun for you on earth.

[1] The hypothetical case, sometimes mentioned by casuists, of one who is convinced that for him salvation outside of religion is impossible, can here safely be passed over as unpractical for young readers.

CHAPTER X
I AM TOO YOUNG

Many a young person, when confronted with the thought of his vocation, puts it out of mind, with the off-hand remark, "Oh, there is plenty of time to consider that; I am too young, and have had no experience of the world." This method of procedure is summary, if not judicious, and it meets with the favor of some parents, who fear, as they think, to lose their children. It was also evidently highly acceptable to Luther, who is quoted by Bellarmine as teaching that no one should enter religious life until he is seventy or eighty years of age.

In deciding a question of this nature, however, we should not allow our prepossessions to bias our judgment, nor take without allowance the opinion of those steeped in worldly wisdom, but lacking in spiritual insight. Father William Humphrey, S.J., in his edition of Suarez's "Religious Life" (page 49), says: "Looking merely to *natural law*, it is lawful at any age freely to offer oneself to the perpetual service of God. There is no natural principle by which should be fixed any certain age for such an act."

Christ did not prescribe any age for those who wished to enter His special service, and He rebuked the apostles for keeping children from Him, saying, "Let the little ones come unto Me." And St. Thomas (Summa, 2a 2æ, Quæst. 189, art. 5), quotes approvingly the comment of Origen on this text, viz.: "We should be careful lest in our superior wisdom we despise the little ones of the Church and prevent them from coming to Jesus." And speaking in the same article of St. Gregory's statement that the Roman nobility offered their sons to St. Benedict to be brought up in the service of God, the Angelic Doctor approves this practice on the principle that "it is good for a man to bear the yoke from his youth," and adds that it is in accord with the usual "custom of setting boys to the duties and occupations in which they are to spend their life."

The remark concerning St. Benedict recalls to mind the interesting fact that in olden times, not only boys of twelve and fourteen became little monks, but that children of three, four or five years of age were brought in their parents' arms and dedicated to the monasteries. According to the "Benedictine Centuries," "the reception of a child in those days was almost as solemn as a profession in our own. His parents carried him to the church. Whilst they wrapped his hand, which held the petition, in the sacred linen of the altar, they promised, in the presence of God and His saints, stability in his name." These children remained during infancy and childhood within the monastery enclosure, and on reaching the age of fourteen, they were given the choice of returning home, if they preferred, or of remaining for life. [1]

The discipline of the Church, which as a wise Mother, she modifies to suit the exigencies of time and place, is somewhat different in our day. The ordinary law now prohibits religious profession before the age of sixteen; and the earliest age at which subjects are commonly admitted is fifteen. Orders which accept younger candidates, in order to train and prepare them for reception, cannot, as a rule, clothe them with the habit. A very recent decree also requires clerical students to have completed four years' study of Latin before admission as novices into any order.

Persons who object to early entrance into religion seem to forget that the young have equal rights with their elders to personal sanctification, and to the use of the means afforded for this purpose by the Church. It is now passed into history, how some misguided individuals forbade frequent Communion to the faithful at large, and altogether excluded from the Holy Table children under twelve or fourteen, and this notwithstanding the plain teaching of the Council of Trent to the contrary. To correct the error, the Holy See was obliged to issue decrees on the subject, which may be styled the charter of Eucharistic freedom for all the faithful, and especially for children. As the Eucharist is not intended solely for the mature or aged, so neither is religious life meant only for the decrepit, or those who have squandered youth and innocence. Its portals are open to all the qualified, and particularly to the young, who wish to bring not a part of their life only, but the *whole* of it, along with youthful enthusiasm and generosity, to God's service.

How many young religious have attained heroic sanctity which would never have been theirs had religion been closed against them by an arbitrary or unreasonable age restriction! A too rigid attitude on this point would have barred those patrons of youth, Aloysius, Stanislaus Kostka and Berchmans, from religion and perhaps even from the honors of the altar. St. Thomas, the great theological luminary of the Church, was offered to the Benedictines when five years old, and he joined the Dominicans at fifteen or sixteen; and St. Rose of Lima made a vow of chastity at five. The Lily of Quito, Blessed Mary Ann, made the three vows of poverty, chastity and obedience before her tenth birthday, and the Little Flower was a Carmelite at fifteen. And uncounted others, who lived and died in the odor of sanctity, dedicated themselves by vow to the perpetual service of God, while still in the fragrance and bloom of childhood or youth.

"What a pity!" some exclaim, when a youth or maid enters religion. "How much better for young people to wait a few years and see something of the world, so they will know what they are giving up." This is ever the comment of the worldly spirit, which aims to crush out entirely spiritual aspirations, and failing in that, to delay their fulfilment indefinitely. And yet the wise do not reason similarly in other matters. One who proposes to cultivate a marked musical talent is never advised to try his hand first at carpentering or tailoring, that he may make an intelligent choice between them. Nor is a promising law student counselled to spend several years in the study of engineering and dentistry, to avoid making a possible mistake. Why then wish a youth, of evident religious inclination, to mingle in the frivolity and gayeties of the world, with the certain risk of imbibing its spirit and losing his spiritual relish? "He who loves the danger," says the Scripture, "will perish in it."

"Yet a vocation should first be tried, and if it cannot resist temptation, it will never prove constant," is the worn but oft-repeated reply. As if a parent would expose his boy to contagion to discover whether his constitution be strong enough to resist it; or place him in the companionship of the depraved to try his virtue and see if it be proof against temptation. No, the tender sprout must be carefully tended, and shielded from wind and storm, until it grows into maturity. In like manner, a young person who desires to serve God, should be placed in an atmosphere favorable to the development of his design, and guarded from sinister influence, until he has acquired stability of purpose and strength of virtue.

There was once in Rome an attractive Cardinal's page of fourteen who possessed a sunny and lively disposition. On a solemn occasion his hasty temper led him to resent the action of another page, and straightway there was a fight. Immediately, the decorous retinue was thrown into confusion, and the Cardinal felt himself disgraced. Peter Ribadeneira, for this was the page's name, did not wait for developments, he foresaw what was coming and fled. Not knowing where to go, he bethought himself of one who was everybody's friend, Ignatius of Loyola, and with soiled face, torn lace and drooping plume, he presented himself before him. Ignatius received him with open arms, and placed him among the novices. Poor Peter had a hard time in the novitiate, as his caprices and boisterousness were always bringing him into trouble. But when grave Fathers frowned, and the novices were scandalized, Peter was ever sure of sympathy and forgiveness from Ignatius, who, in the end, was gratified to see the boy develop into an able, learned and holy religious. Peter's vocation was occasioned by his fight, certainly an unpropitious beginning, but he must have ever been grateful that, when he applied to Ignatius, he was not turned away until he had become older and more sedate.

Parents or spiritual directors, who, under the pretext of trying a vocation, put off for two or three years an aspirant who seems dowered with all necessary qualities, can scarcely justify themselves in the eyes of God, such a method being calculated to destroy, not prove, a vocation. To detain for a few months, however, one who conceives a sudden notion to enter religion, for the purpose of discovering whether his intention is serious, and not merely a passing whim, is only in accordance with the ordinary rules of prudence. In connection with this point, the words of bluff and hearty St. Jerome, who never seemed to grow old or lose the buoyancy of youth, are often quoted. Giving advice to one whom he wished to quit the world, he wrote, "Wait not even to untie the rope that holds your boat at anchor—cut it." (M. P. L., t. 26, c. 549.) And Christ's reply to the young man, whom He had invited to follow Him, and who asked leave to go first and bury his father, was equally terse: "Let the dead bury their own dead." (Luke ix: 60.)

In a booklet entitled "Questions on Vocations," published in 1913, by a Priest of the Congregation of the Mission, the question is asked, "Do not a larger percentage persevere when subjects enter the religious state late in life?" And the answer is given: "No; the records of five of the largest communities of Sisters in the United States show that a much larger percentage of subjects persevere among those who enter between the ages of sixteen and twenty, than among those who enter when they are older. When persons are twenty years of age, or older, their characters are more set; their minds are less pliable; it is harder to unbend and remould them. The young are more readily formed to religious discipline."

In concluding this chapter on the appropriate age for entrance into religious life, it may be said that, after reaching the prescribed age of fifteen, the sooner an otherwise properly qualified person enters the nearer he seems to approach the ideals and traditionary practice of the Church, and the better he will provide for his own spiritual welfare.

[1] It would seem that for the space of two centuries, this freedom of choice was not offered them.

CHAPTER XI
THE PRIESTHOOD

The High Priest of the New Law, St. Paul tells the Hebrews, is Christ. And the Christian priesthood, which He instituted, is a participation and extension of His office and ministry. The commemoration of the same sacrifice which was once offered upon the cross for the sins of the world is daily renewed on our altars from the rising to the setting of the sun. The Christian priest, in the language of spiritual writers, is "another Christ," taking His place amongst men, perpetually renewing, as it were, the Incarnation in the Sacrifice of the Mass, preaching the word, and applying the fruits of Redemption through the channels of the sacraments.

In common estimation, the dignity of a man is reckoned by the character of the office he fills or the duties entrusted to him. Judged by this standard, no worldly dignity can compare with that of the priesthood, whose authority comes from God, and whose powers, transcending earth, reach back to heaven. "Speak not of the royal purple," says St. Chrysostom, "of diadems, of golden vestures—these are but shadows, frailer than the flowers of spring, compared to the power and privileges of the priesthood."

And whence arises, we may ask, this incomparable dignity of the priest? First of all, from his power to roll back the heavens, and bring down upon the altar the Majesty of the Deity, attended by an angelic train. "The Blessed Virgin," St. Vincent Ferrer informs us, "opened heaven only once, the priest does so at every Mass." Exalted is the sovereignty of kings who rule a nation, but more sublime the power which commands the King of kings, and is obeyed. Who could conceive, did not Faith teach it, that mortal man were capable of elevation to such a pitch of glory? No wonder St. Chrysostom was betrayed by this thought into the rhapsody: "When you behold the Lord immolated and lying on the altar, and the priest standing over the sacrifice and praying and all the people empurpled by that precious blood, do you imagine that you are still on earth amongst men and not rather rapt up to heaven?"

The second great prerogative of the priest is to forgive sins. Christ having one day said to a paralytic, "Man, thy sins are forgiven thee" (Luke v: 20), some of the bystanders marvelled, thinking within themselves, "Who can forgive sins, but God alone?" Yea, truly is this a Divine power, but these critics failed to comprehend the Divinity of Christ, and that all power was given to Him in heaven and on earth. And His power to remit sins has descended to the priest, in the imposition of hands. At Christ's will lepers were cleansed, and once more felt the pulsation of health tingling through their veins; but more wondrous still the word of the priest which causes the scales of the leprosy of sin to fall from the stricken soul, and restores to it the pristine vigor and beauty of sanctifying grace. As keeper of the keys, the priest stands warder of heaven, locking or unlocking its doors to the dust-begrimed pilgrims of earth.

Sublime, then, is the priestly dignity, even beyond human comprehension. But one thing we realize, and the saints with clearer vision perceive, that high virtue is demanded of him whose life is spent in the antechamber of heaven. St. Catharine of Sienna, in a letter to one newly ordained, tells him, "The ministers whom the Sovereign Goodness has chosen to be His Christs ought to be angels, not men . . . they in truth discharge the office of angels." "What purity," says a Father of the Church, "what piety shall we require of a priest? Think what those hands ought to be which perform such a ministry; what that tongue which pronounces those words." No sanctity or purity of soul, then, is beyond the aspirations of one whose heaven-born privilege it is to enter the Holy of Holies, to dispense the mysteries of faith, and exercise the "ministry of reconciliation."

A most important function of the ministry is the care of souls. Christ's mission was to save; He was the Good Shepherd, who traveled about preaching to the people, who were like "sheep without a shepherd." And to His Apostles and their successors He gave the solemn charge "to feed His lambs." And this injunction of the Divine Master has been held sacred by the Church throughout its existence. Wherever in the world to-day dwell true believers, there are to be found priests to care for them.

The priest is truly the father of the people committed to him. He must become all things to all men, rejoicing with the joyful, and weeping with the sorrowful. The infants he must receive into the Church, generating in them the life of grace, guarding them as they grow up, and instructing them in doctrine and discipline. To him the bridal couple come for the nuptial benediction; and when sickness and trouble and want invade the household it is to their father in Christ the faithful look for support and encouragement. He is the consoler of all, and he bears the burdens of all. And when the angel of death hovers over his charge, the priest repairs to the bedside of the departing one, to strengthen him for the last journey; and, finally, when the soul has departed, he commits the body to hallowed ground, there to await the resurrection.

The priest, then, must be of heroic mould to satisfy the demands made upon him; he must be ready to endure hunger and cold and weariness, contradictions from within and without, labors by night and day. But the Lord is his inheritance, and for His sake he is willing to endure all the crosses and trials that bear upon him. How splendidly the clergy of our country have responded to their responsibilities is attested by the flourishing state of religion, by the magnificent churches, the well-developed Catholic school system, and the numerous other Church activities about us. Every thoroughly organized parish or mission means the life of at least one priest sacrificed in its formation—the commingling of his sweat and labors with the cement that binds together its material and spiritual stones. But could a life be better spent? What more fitting monument could be left to posterity than a spiritual structure built on Christ and enduring as the foundation on which it rests?

Who, then, may aspire to the glorious career of the priesthood? Is it open to all, or must one await the striking manifestation of the Divine Will inviting him to it? Should he not say, "The priesthood is too exalted for my weakness and unworthiness"? While humility is laudable, it should not bar any one who has the requisite virtue and talent, together with an upright intention, from entering this high estate. Everything depends on one's qualifications and motives. Others will pass judgment on the qualifications, but each one must scrutinize his own motives. If a youth desires the priesthood for natural reasons, to lead an easy life or one honorable in the eyes of men, to attain fame or station, his motives are wrong, or at least, too imperfect to carry him far on the rugged road before him. But if he be swayed by supernatural desires, such as the service of God, his own sanctification or the help of his neighbor, his ambition is praiseworthy. One who is conscious, then, of rectitude of purpose and hopeful with the divine assistance of living up to its obligations, may aspire, without scruple, to the priesthood, the highest of dignities and the greatest of careers open to man.

One day our Lord, instructing His disciples before sending them to preach His coming, said: "The harvest, indeed, is great, but the laborers are few. Pray ye therefore the Lord of the harvest, that he send laborers into his harvest" (Luke x: 2). And this has been the cry through all the ages—"Send laborers into the harvest!" The Church has always needed good spiritual laborers, men and women, who would be willing to work for God and their neighbor, to extend the Kingdom of God, and this is true to-day of our own beloved country. A host of spiritual laborers is scattered over our land, but the cry is ever repeated, "We need more, the work is too great for our efforts, and all the harvest is not being garnered."

Will you, dear reader, make one more worker in God's field, one more reaper of His harvest that is ripe and falling to the ground because there are none to gather it?

CHAPTER XII
THE TEACHER'S AUREOLE

As the acquaintance of young people with religious is frequently limited to their teachers, they are sometimes inclined to identify in their minds the profession of teaching with religious life. And since some feel a diffidence or repugnance in committing themselves to a teaching career, they extend this aversion to the religious state itself. We have shown, however, in a previous chapter that there is great variety and diversity of occupation in religious orders, so that all tastes and inclinations can find congenial exercise in them.

Still, it is probably true, that the great majority of religious men and women are found in the class-room, and this for the good and sufficient reason that Christian education is the paramount need of the day, and the work on which the future of the Church chiefly depends. The young who, perhaps, are tempted to look upon teaching as an obscure employment and a monotonous grind, will do well to reflect that in our time it is considered

21

so honorable a profession that hundreds of thousands, even of those outside the Church, deliberately choose it as the best and most favorable career for the play of their talents.

The professors of our noted universities command the respect and deference of the community, and to them the public look for the solution of the constantly arising civic and social problems. They are regarded as the natural leaders of thought, and are expected to guide and direct popular movements affecting the well-being of society. And this public esteem, is extended in due proportion to all who are engaged in education, for it is universally realized that the standard of morality and intelligence, which is to obtain in the commonwealth, will depend largely on the training given to the young. The teacher is directly employed in the making of good citizens, which is a more important business than the extension of manufactures or commerce. He is setting the ideals according to which the Republic must stand or fall.

And, for persons of refined or intellectual tastes, the instruction of youth must be a pleasurable employment. It is inviting to deal with the young and innocent, who are eager to learn, ambitious to excel, and who in return for their instructor's solicitude, give him unstinted affection and gratitude, and render him loyal obedience and respect. In the teacher's hands is the moulding and shaping of character, the direction of talents which may illumine society. And can any sphere of action be more elevated, more grateful than this?

And then, too, the educator is constantly engaged in the things of the mind, in study, and the discovery of new truths or new applications of old ones, and in imparting his knowledge to fresh, bright intelligences. Nothing is so fascinating to a person of intellectual bent as the pursuit and attainment of truth, and this is the steady occupation of the teacher. Is not the outlook of such a life infinitely wider and more refreshing than the dull routine of business, the noisy rumble of a factory or the sordid dealings of commerce?

But it is principally from the spiritual point of view that education is considered by the Church and religious congregations. The mandate of Christ, "Go ye forth and teach all nations," laid the charge of teaching upon His Church; and on the pastors it devolves to see that the faithful are instructed in Christian doctrines and obligations. To rightfully carry out its mission, the Church has always felt obliged to insist that the education of its children be permeated with religion, and in fulfilment of this duty it has established parochial schools throughout our country, where the young, while acquiring secular science, can at the same time be grounded in the faith and trained to virtuous lives.

It can be said, then, that the religious who conduct these schools share in the apostolic mission of the Church. Every catechetical instruction, every word of exhortation or encouragement to right living and doing which is given in the class-room, is a participation by the teacher in the pastorate of souls, in the announcing and preaching of the Gospel, in the spreading of the Kingdom of God. Without the aid of the school, the pastor ordinarily could not properly teach the young their prayers and catechism, prepare them for the sacraments, and equip them for the manifold exigencies of life.

"Religious education is our most distinctive work," says Archbishop Spalding, of Peoria. "It gives us a place apart in the life of the country. It is indispensable to the welfare and progress of the Church in the United States, and will be recognized in the end as the most vital contribution to American civilization. Fortunate are they, who by words or deeds confirm our faith in the need of Catholic schools; and yet more fortunate are they who, while they inspire our teachers with new courage and zeal, awaken in the young, to whom God has given a heart and a mind, an efficacious desire to devote themselves to the little ones whom Christ loves. What better work, in the present time, can any of us do than foster vocations to our Brotherhoods and Sisterhoods, whose special mission is teaching?"

And Brother Azarias assures us that "There is not in this world among human callings a more sacred one than that of moulding souls to higher and better things."

Bishop Byrne, of Nashville, has well said: "The office of teaching has an advantage in some respects over the priesthood. The teachers are constantly with their pupils, shaping their souls, coloring them, informing them, making them instinct with life and motives, and giving them high ideals and worthy aspirations. In all this their work is akin to that of the confessor."

The need of more teaching Brothers and Sisters is particularly urgent and pressing, as the number of pupils is increasing proportionately faster than the number of religious subjects, and the dearth of teachers prevents the opening of new schools in many places where they are demanded, and also hinders the development of the existing schools. This is the opinion of Bishop Alerding, who wrote: "The Church is being hampered in her work of educating her youth because the number of teachers, Brothers and Sisters, is inadequate." And Bishop McQuaid did not hesitate to say that, "the most pressing want of the Church in America at the present time is that of Brothers to assist in teaching our boys."

In this connection we may observe that some virtuous and self-effacing souls, after the example of St. Francis of Assisi, have a dread of assuming the responsibilities of the priesthood, and there are many others who are debarred from aspiring to that dignity by insufficiency of education. Young men of either of these classes have a splendid opportunity before them to serve God by joining a teaching congregation of Brothers.

Finally, as an encouragement to Christian teachers in their glorious apostolate, let them remember the great reward awaiting their unselfish labors. The Book of Daniel (xii: 3), tells us that "They who instruct many to justice shall shine as stars for all eternity." The inspired writer compares teachers to the stars of heaven, for as the latter illumine the darkness of night, so they who instruct others dispel the darkness of ignorance by shedding the rays of wisdom and knowledge into the minds of their disciples. But there is a deeper meaning in this text, for according to the interpretation of theologians, it contains the assurance to those who teach others their duty, of a special reward or golden crown in heaven, called the Doctor's or Teacher's Aureole. The exact nature of this privilege, whether it is a special gift of loving God or a distinctive garb of glory, we do not know, but as the martyrs and virgins have their special aureole, so will teachers have theirs.

Father Croiset exclaims: "Oh! the beautiful and rich crowns which God prepares for a religious who inspires little children with a horror of vice and a love of virtue! . . . What sweet consolation will be experienced at the moment of death by the religious when he beholds coming to his aid those souls whom he has helped to save." And we may faintly conceive the transport of one who enters heaven accompanied by the resplendent retinue of those whom he has brought with him from earth.

This chapter would not be complete without a word of encouragement to those young men and women whose education is so deficient that they feel incompetent to teach, and so turn away in sadness from the portals of religion, thinking there is no room for them within. Such persons should know that any one who is skilled in a trade, such as that of carpentering, painting, tailoring, or sewing, can be of the greatest utility and acceptability to a community. And there are many offices of a domestic nature, such as that of porter, sacristan, refectorian and steward, which require little preparatory training and can be filled by any one of intelligence and good will.

Nor should persons engaged in such duties entertain the notion that they will not share in the full spiritual privileges of the Order; for by the assistance they give to the other members they are contributing to the end and aim of the Institute and communicate in all the good works performed by it. An edifying incident, illustrative of this point, is told of a famous preacher who moved hearts in a wondrous fashion, and when he was tempted to self-complacency in his success, it was revealed to him that the results of his preaching were due, not to his own eloquence or zeal, but to the prayers of the unobserved lay-brother, who always sat at the foot of the pulpit, telling his beads for the efficacy of the sermon.

CHAPTER XIII
SHOWING THE WAY

When young people read or hear of persons entering religious life, they are apt to say, "Oh, it is easy for them, because they are holy; but it is impossible for me who have so little virtue!" But, as a matter of fact, these religious have the same passions and temptations to overcome, the same flesh and blood, as ourselves, and it was only by conquering themselves, and struggling with their lower inclinations, that they obtained the victory.

A boy was standing one day at a country railway station in the United States, when he met an older boy with whom he engaged in conversation. His casual acquaintance confided to him that he was going off to college to prepare for entrance into a certain religious Order; and he urged the younger lad to accompany him for the same purpose. But the latter replied, "Oh! they wouldn't have me, for I am poor, uneducated and every way unfit." The other insisted, however, and finally prevailed on him to board with him the incoming train. They repaired to the superior of the religious Order, who received them kindly, and sent them both to a boarding school. After a short time the senior student was caught stealing, and dismissed from the college. His whilom companion, however, persevered in his good design, achieved honors in his studies, and finally becoming a religious and a priest, he is today doing effective work in the vineyard of the Lord.

A story is told of a religious who gave a letter to a young man, in which he recommended him as a suitable candidate for his Order, bidding him present the letter to the superior, who lived at a distance. The young man, desirous of joining the Order, started on his journey with a companion named Mathias, who had no notion of becoming a religious. On the way, the would-be religious changed his mind, and abandoning his project, gave the letter to Mathias, who was ignorant of its contents, requesting him to bring it to the superior. The superior read the letter, and thinking the recommendation referred to Mathias, said to him, "Very well, you may go to the novitiate, and put on the habit." Mathias wondered, but obeyed, entered the novitiate, and became a holy religious.

St. Bernard, Abbot of Clairvaux, and the foremost man of his age, was so handsome and attractive in youth, that the evil-minded laid snares against his chastity. To escape their wiles he determined to enter the Cistercian monastery of Citeaux. His father and brothers endeavored to dissuade him from his purpose, but instead, by his fervid exhortations, he induced four of his brothers and others, to the number of thirty, to enter with him. As the party was leaving home, little Nivard, the sole remaining boy of the family, was at play with some companions. Guido, the eldest of the brothers, embraced him and said, "My dear Nivard, we are going, and this castle and lands will all be yours." The child, "with wisdom beyond his years," the chronicler tells us, "replied, 'what, are you taking heaven for yourselves, and leaving earth to me? The division is not fair.'" And from that day nothing could pacify the boy, until he was permitted to join his brothers.

St. Alphonsus Liguori, who is said to have always preserved his baptismal innocence, was so brilliant a student that at the age of sixteen he had obtained two degrees in the University of Naples. Entering on the practice of the law, he one day in a trial before the court, by an oversight, misstated the evidence. His attention being called to his error, he was so overwhelmed with shame and confusion at his apparent lack of truthfulness, that on returning home he exclaimed, "World, I know you now, Courts, you shall never see me more." And for three days he refused food. He then determined to become a priest, and in the ministry he attained great sanctity. He founded the well-known Congregation of the Most Holy Redeemer, commonly called the Redemptorists; and for his voluminous doctrinal writings, Pius IX declared him a Doctor of the universal Church.

The story of the entrance of St. Stanislaus Kostka into religion reads like a romance. His father, a Polish nobleman, had placed him and his older brother, Paul, at the Jesuit College in Vienna. When Stanislaus was fifteen years of age he applied for admission into the Jesuit Order, but as he had not the consent of his father, the superior feared to take him. An illness supervened, and the Blessed Virgin came to cure him, and giving the child Jesus into his arms, said to him, "You must end your days in the Society that bears my Son's name; you must become a Jesuit."

Notwithstanding the vision, poor Stanislaus was again refused by the Jesuit superior. Not knowing what other step to take, he thought that by traveling four hundred miles to Augsburg, in Germany, the Jesuit Provincial of that province, who at the time was Blessed Peter Canisius, might receive him, for his jurisdiction seemed beyond the influence of Senator Kostka. If again rejected in Augsburg, he was determined to walk eight hundred miles farther to Rome, where he felt sure of securing his heart's desire. Accordingly, one August morning he rose early and telling his servant that he was going out, bade him at the same time inform his brother Paul not to expect him for dinner. With light and joyous heart he started on his journey, and at the first opportunity exchanged his fine clothes for the disguise of a pilgrim's staff and tunic.

When Paul awoke and learned that Stanislaus was gone for the day, he was surprised, but attributed it to some new pious freak. But as the day wore on, and the shades of evening gathered, with no tidings of his brother, consternation seized Paul, for he realized that his irascible and powerful father would hold him responsible for the safety of the younger boy, whom he loved with a passionate and unbounded affection. Accordingly servants were dispatched in every direction to seek for the truant, but no tidings could be obtained. The conclusion gradually forced itself upon all that Stanislaus had fled, and Paul determined to pursue him and bring him back. For some reason, suspicion was aroused that the runaway had taken the road to Augsburg, and a carriage with two stout horses was ordered for early dawn on the morrow.

Along the highway to Augsburg flew the equipage containing Paul and three companions. Meanwhile, little Stanislaus was trudging bravely along, putting all his confidence in God, when he suddenly heard the rapid beat of horses' hoofs behind him. Suspecting what it meant, he quickly entered a by-lane, and the occupants of the carriage rushed by without seeing, or at least, recognizing, him in his disguise.

Stanislaus continued his pilgrimage in peace, begging his way, for he had no money, and after two weeks, he saw, with inexpressible joy, the roofs and spires of Augsburg gleaming in the setting sun. At last he had reached the haven of rest, and with a bounding heart, the weary boy knocked at the door of the Jesuit college. But alas, for all his hopes! the provincial had gone to Dillingen. The Fathers urged him to stay and rest with them until the provincial's return, but Stanislaus would brook no delay. At once he wended his way toward Dillingen, which he soon reached, and when he knelt at the feet of Blessed Canisius, two saints were face to face. The superior pressed the boy to his heart, and kept him in the college for a few weeks. But as both the elder and younger saint thought Germany still too near the influence of his father for safety, Stanislaus, in company with two religious, set out on a further exhausting walk of eight hundred miles to Rome, where he was received as a Jesuit novice by the General of the Order, St. Francis Borgia.

The angelic boy had at last finished his long pilgrimages, he had entered the earthly paradise for which he had yearned, and for which he had forsaken home, rank and country. But the happiness of religion he soon exchanged for the joys of heaven, for before completing his eighteenth year, and while still a novice, he closed his eyes on this world to open them in company with Mary and the angels on the Beatific Vision.

CHAPTER XIV
THE PARENTS' PART

The home is the nursery of vocations. Most religious can trace the beginnings of their resolve to leave all to the influence of saintly parents and a Christian home. If the parents cultivate faith, charity and industry the fragrance of these virtues will cling round the walls of their dwelling, and perfume the lives of their children.

Every Christian home should be a convent in miniature, filled with the same spirit, productive of the same virtues. It should be a cloister, forbidding entrance to the world and its vanities, and harboring within gentle peace and happiness. Poverty should dwell there, not in the narrower meaning of distress and want, but in the wider acceptation of simplicity, frugality and temperance as opposed to extravagance, display and ostentation. Purity, too, should reign as queen of the hearth, regulating the glance of the eye, the conversation, and even the thoughts of the occupants. And union and harmony of wills, without which the idea of home is inconceivable, can come only through obedience which binds the children to parents, wife to husband, and all to God.

But, unfortunately, this is not always the case. From many domiciles peace and tranquillity have fled, giving place to frivolity, vanity and worldliness and all their attendant train of vices. How many parents, deceived by the wisdom of the flesh, seek their own gratification in all things, and denying their children nothing that luxury or extravagance craves, pamper and spoil them by indulging their every whim. To train up the young to the steady and uncompromising fulfilment of duty is the only means to produce a hardy and sturdy generation of men and women, whose fidelity can be relied on in the trials and emergencies of after-life.

But some fathers and mothers, when their children call for bread, reverse the parable by giving them a stone, and when they ask for an egg, give them a scorpion. We can imagine with what righteous indignation Our Lord would have denounced such a mode of action. Foolish parents even of limited means dress their girls in expensive and gaudy apparel, which not only offends against taste and economy, but sometimes transgresses the laws of modesty and decency. Familiarity between the sexes is permitted and encouraged by doting and foolish mothers, who introduce their sons and daughters to juvenile society functions, receptions, parties and unbecoming dances; so that children who should be at their lessons or playing healthful games with suitable companions, are taught to affect society manners after the most approved fashion of their silly elders. Persons of this stamp may prepare for a rude awakening, for the day of reckoning for themselves and children will be sure and terrible.

Many parents, while indeed quite solicitous according to their lights, for the temporal good of their offspring, training them to a trade or profession, or settling them in marriage, devote but little thought to their spiritual welfare. They dread a vocation in their family as a catastrophe. It would be well, indeed, for persons of this character to ponder the words of the Pastoral Letter of the Second Council of Baltimore: "We fear that the fault lies in great part with many parents, who instead of fostering the desire so natural to the youthful heart, of dedicating itself to the service of God's sanctuary, but too often impart to their children their own worldly-mindedness, and seek to influence their choice of a state of life by unduly exaggerating the difficulties and dangers of the priestly calling, and painting in too glowing colors the advantages of a secular life."

How much better it were for parents to propose to the young the promise of Our Lord, "And every one that hath left house, or brothers or sisters or father or mother or wife or children or lands for my name, shall receive a hundredfold, and possess life everlasting." (Matt. xix: 29.) Many a one, whose wayward child has brought dishonor and shame to the family, realizes when all too late the happiness that might have been his had such a child only elected the religious state.

Instead of throwing obstacles in the way of a vocation, those who are appreciative of spiritual things feel honored that God has chosen one of their family circle for His special service. Persons whose sons obtain high position in the army, court or government employ, take a just pride in the distinction thus attained, but such temporal honors cannot be compared with the singular privilege of serving in God's own courts, and dwelling within His sanctuary. Bishop Schrembs, of Toledo, aptly advises pastors "to teach young parents that the service of God is even more glorious than that of country, for as St. Jerome says, 'Such a service establishes ties of relationship between the family and Jesus Christ Himself.'"

Nor do parents, as they sometimes fear, lose a son or daughter who enters religion. One who marries is in a certain sense lost to the parent, for the responsibilities of his new state of life so absorb his energies as to leave him but little opportunity to concern himself about his old home. And frequently distance entirely severs his connection with it. But one who enters God's house does not contract new family alliances, his heart remains free, and though separated from parents, his affection is always true to them, he thinks of them as in his childhood days, and he never ceases to importune the blessings of heaven upon them.

In fact, we may say that a vocation is not strictly an individual, but rather a family possession. A call to God implies sacrifice on the part of the family, as well as of the individual, for while he gives up parents, brothers and sisters, they, too, must part with him. And as they share in the renunciation, they participate also in its merit and reward. In God's household the religious represents his family, he works and prays by proxy for them, and they share in his graces and good deeds. Is it not a matter of daily experience that the family of a religious, particularly the parents, receive abundant graces, that God leads them in various ways to greater fidelity in His service, to a love of prayer and higher perfection? Parents of religious frequently become religious themselves at heart, and though not clothed with the habit, they share in the "hundredfold" promised to the child.

"It is the glory of a large and happy Catholic family to produce a vocation," says Rev. Joseph Rickaby, S.J. "A sound Catholic is glad to have brother or sister, uncle or aunt, or cousin or child, 'who has pleased God and is found no more' in the ordinary walks of life, because God hath taken and translated him to something higher and better."

Parents and teachers, then, who do not hesitate to incline the minds of children to a professional career, should have no fear also to direct their thoughts to higher things. To praise in the family circle the priestly or religious life, to express the hope and desire that one or more of the children may have the great happiness of such a profession, to offer them daily in prayer to God, to train them to piety and devotion, these are all praiseworthy in a father or mother, and if faithfully practiced in all families would doubtless greatly increase the number of God's chosen servants.

Anything approaching coercion or excessive urging should, of course, be avoided, because moral violence should not be done to the child's will. But the remark sometimes made by well-meaning mothers, "O, I would not say a word to influence my child towards religion, for fear of interfering with God's work," shows a lamentable ignorance of the nature of a vocation. One might almost as well say, "O, I am careful not to contribute to the building of a church, because if God wants it built, He will not need any help." If all persons thought thus, such a church would be long in building.

Most of God's works require our cooperation. He designs them and we must carry them out. Many a great project has depended on a timely word, or on the exertions of some man who rose to the occasion. Andrew and John were sent to Our Lord by St. John the Baptist, and they became apostles; and if Andrew had not "found his brother Simon and brought him to Jesus," who knows whether Christ would not have found it necessary to appoint another head of the Church in place of Simon Peter?

To parents, then, belongs the singular privilege of training their children to tender piety, of directing their thoughts to spiritual things; and fidelity to this trust will give us a glorious generation of men and women ready to risk all, to sacrifice all in the service of their Creator.

CHAPTER XV
A PARTING WORD

Now, dear reader, that you and the writer have kept company thus far, he is reluctant to part from you. But if you perceive within you the germ of a vocation, he begs you not to crush it. If in your heart there is a spark of that celestial fire, which may be fanned to a consuming flame of divine love, keep it burning.

Preserve your soul, oh! so perfectly from the slightest touch of evil, remembering that the least deliberate venial sin stains it more than we can comprehend. Above all, cherish holy purity, that exquisite ornament of youth, which, like a polished gem, may so easily lose its lustre. Guard the avenues of your soul, your sight and hearing and the other senses, through which contamination from without is always seeking to enter and defile the beauty of God's handiwork. About us is an atmosphere of worldliness, which we imperceptibly breathe in from the words of companions, from the printed page, and the example of the careless. Shun companionship with the frivolous, vanity of dress, and that indiscriminate reading which only feeds an idle curiosity. The theatres of our day are especially dangerous to virtue, and he who stays away from them entirely, will consult his own advantage, as well as please God.

In this soft and luxurious age the popular trend is to self-gratification in all its forms. But the true Christian must ever strive against corrupt nature, if he would not be carried away by the stream of voluptuousness. Self-denial is the watchword of Christianity. All are called to the practice of penance in some shape or form, the best usually being the exact performance of duty. The young of school age will find a strong shelter from temptation in the scrupulous and enthusiastic performance of their daily tasks and lessons. That small boy had caught the true spirit, who used to rise early, to prepare himself, as he said, for the "missionary" life, to which he aspired.

A material help for boys to prepare for future life, is to serve at the altar. He who sacrifices his morning sleep, overcoming sloth, to minister to the priest at Mass, is already, by a privilege, fulfilling the functions of one of the minor orders, that of the acolyte. The devout server at Mass shares in its graces next to the celebrant, and more than the ordinary faithful who assist at it; and many an altar-boy, as he glided about the sanctuary, mingling with the invisible angels who hovered around the Victim of sacrifice, has felt the seeds of vocation sprouting in his soul.

Devotion to the Mother of God should also be a characteristic of youth. She sympathizes with us, as only a mother can, in all our difficulties and trials. She fully appreciates what we have to contend with, she sees our weakness, the strength of our passions, the temptations we encounter, and she is eager to throw about us the mantle of her protection, if we will only ask her. Never a day should pass without our commending ourselves earnestly to her motherly heart, for she is even more interested in our welfare than we ourselves. She is powerful to aid us, since all good things come to us through her; and she will choose for her devout clients the career in which they may best serve God.

By a strange perversion of mind, we often seek to unravel the perplexities of life, without recourse to prayer. When involved in business anxieties, men spend days of worry in wrestling with them, without perhaps asking the Father of Lights for guidance. And the young also, who must settle for themselves their future career, frequently strive to do so, without the help of heaven. They perhaps consult human advisers, but fail to consult God, the best of counsellors, Who alone can see behind the veil of the future, and infallibly tell what is best for us.

In coming to any important decision, light and strength are needed, light to know the pathway of duty, and strength to follow it. On account of the obscurities and half-lights of our intellect, we perceive but dimly, and often fail to discern the true from the false. The illumination of the white light of Truth is needed to flood the dark recesses of the mind. And even when the truth stands clearly revealed, we are often too indolent or enervated to embrace it; we need the tonic of resolution and courage, which can be infused into us only from on high.

The trustful child of God should, day by day, commend his future into the hands of his heavenly Father, praying Him to shape his life and career. Each one has his own talents, one or many, but he cannot hope to trade or barter with them in a fruitful way unless the Giver of them bless his efforts. Our constant prayer, then, should be for the fulfilment of God's will in our regard, with the lively faith that whatever we ask will be granted.

And of all prayers and devotions, can any be more efficacious or salutary than the frequent reception of the Holy Eucharist? Our Holy Father, Pius X, desires the boys and girls of the whole world to be nourished daily, from the tenderest years, with the Bread of Life, that they may wax strong in the spiritual life, and grow up virile Christians. One Holy Communion, received fervently, should be sufficient to sanctify a soul and awake in it the desire of closest union with Christ, of self-immolation on the altar of Divine Love.

Then what of the soul which is daily nourished with the "Wheat of the Elect and the Wine that springeth forth Virgins?" (Zach. ix: 17.) Holy Communion has been styled the "Marriage Supper of the Lamb," wherein Christ caresses the soul, communicates to it sweetest secrets, and touching it with the ardent flames of His own Heart, purifies it from attachment to creatures, and sets it aglow with the white heat of charity. The frequent communicant, then, is surest of knowing and doing God's will.

In conclusion, the writer may be allowed to indulge the hope that more than one reader may be impelled to aspire to the virgin's aureole, the special privilege of joining the one hundred and forty-four thousand, whom St. John, in the vision of the Apocalypse, saw following the Lamb, whithersoever He went, and singing a canticle that none else could sing, "because they were virgins."

Go now, little book, fly away to some perplexed soul who is anxious to discover the secrets of the Divine Will; and whisper it a message of peace and consolation, telling it that, "Eye hath not seen, nor ear heard, nor hath it entered into the heart of man, what things God hath prepared for them that love Him." (I Cor. ii: 9.)

PRAYER FOR THE RIGHT CHOICE OF A STATE OF LIFE.

O Thou, the God of wisdom and counsel, Who dost perceive in my heart a sincere desire of pleasing Thee alone, and of conforming myself entirely to Thy most holy will in the choice of my state of life, grant me, I beseech Thee, through the intercession of the Blessed Virgin, my mother, and of my patron saints, especially St. Joseph and St. Aloysius, the grace to know what state of life I should choose, and when known to embrace it, so that I may seek and spread therein Thy glory, work out my salvation, and merit that reward in heaven which Thou hast promised to those who fulfill Thy divine will. Amen.

An indulgence of three hundred days, once a day, for the above prayer, granted by Pope Pius X, May 2, 1905.

Made in the USA
Las Vegas, NV
13 July 2023

74661426R00020